Summary of

D1742939

The 30-Day Ketogenic Cleanse

Maria Emmerich

Conversation Starters

By BookHabits

Bonus Downloads
*Get Free Books with **<u>Any Purchase</u>** of* Conversation Starters!

Every purchase comes with a FREE download!

Add spice to any conversation
Never run out of things to say
Spend time with those you love

Get it Now

<u>or Click Here.</u>

Scan Your Phone

Tips for Using Conversation Starters:

EVERY GOOD BOOK CONTAINS A WORLD FAR DEEPER THAN the surface of its pages. Questions herein are designed to bring us beneath the surface of the page and invite us into the world that lives on. These questions can be used to:

- Foster a deeper understanding of the book
- Promote an atmosphere of discussion for groups
- Assist in the study of the book, either individually or corporately
- Explore unseen realms of the book as never seen before

Table of Contents

Introducing *The 30-Day Ketogenic Cleanse* 6

Discussion Questions 14

Introducing the Author 35

Fireside Questions... 42

Quiz Questions 53

Quiz Answers... 66

Ways to Continue Your Reading 67

Introducing *The 30-Day Ketogenic Cleanse*

*T*he 30 Day Ketogenic Cleanse is a new book from Maria Emmerich. It is perfect for people who are trying to restart their ketogenic diet after the fell off or people who are just starting the ketogenic diet. The first thirty days of any lifestyle change are the most difficult and challenging, which is why Emmerich has written this guide to the ketogenic diet for the first thirty days of switching to it. The ketogenic diet is built upon the idea that the body will burn fat, also called ketones, by eating proper foods and getting energy from protein and fat rather than carbohydrates. In the first thirty days, cravings may start, the body may have a difficult time adapting to the new way of eating, and many people do not feel their best. This leads to the temptation to give up on the diet before they can truly see the benefits the diet can offer them. The best part is that people do not have to starve in order to see results, and Maria Emmerich provides the recipes that are satisfying and designed to keep cravings away. There are also tips offered throughout the book that will help people get through the period of adjusting to the ketogenic lifestyle.

Emmerich was inspired to write *The 30 Day Ketogenic Cleanse* because she struggled with her weight and eating in her childhood and into her adult years, as well. When she was a teenager, Emmerich recalls trying on a jacket that belonged to her friend. A boy walked by as she was trying it on and called her a "fat girl" wearing a small coat. This experience was what started what Emmerich calls her "wake up call."

Emmerich became frustrated that she was struggling to lose weight. She was exercising, but still unable to see the amount of weight loss she wanted. She decided at that point in her life, it was time to start factoring in nutrition to her weight loss plan. She was about to go out into the world and tell people how to be healthy, as well, and decided it was to practice what she was about to preach.

Emmerich classified herself as a "fat restrictor." She was taught that eating fat free was the best way to drop pounds and inches. When she first started eating real fat for the first time, it was scary for her. She watched her health begin to improve when she began eating this fat, however. She was calmer throughout the day and had deeper sleep. She suddenly understood all of the reasons that staying away from fat was not helping her. This experience reframed how she thought about food. She now knew that foods hat tasted good did not make a person fat.

By following a ketogenic diet, Emmerich says she was able to heal her mitochondria. She became educated about the hormones insulin and leptin.

Through education and the correct diet for her body, Emmerich was also able to change her biochemistry to make her body respond to insulin and leptin again. The best part of following the ketogenic diet, according to Emmerich, is that she no longer felt deprived of nutrients. In the end, she lost more weight than she had originally planned. Emmerich believes that everyone can benefit from changing to a ketogenic lifestyle.

As for the typical diets recommended by dietitians, Emmerich uses biology to back up that the ketogenic diet is actually healthy. In response to claims that people should stay away from cholesterol and saturated fats, Emmerich points out that breast milk is made up of mainly cholesterol and saturated fat. It is unlikely, in Emmerich's opinion, that breast milk was created in order to hurt or cause babies to be unhealthy. Instead, it helps them grow, helps create healthy hormones in their bodies, helps to create the myelin sheath around their cells so that their nerve cells can communicate with each other properly, and it helps their brains become healthier.

Through *The 30 Day Ketogenic Cleanse*, Emmerich hopes that she can reach out to as many people as possible. She wants to help people so that they do not have to suffer with health problems or die an early death that could have been prevented by proper nutrition. Emmerich says that her book is for people who have previously tried to follow a ketogenic diet without seeing the results they wanted. It is also for people who have wanted to try the ketogenic diet for a while. Emmerich's book can help both groups of people find success through this change in lifestyle.

In *The 30 Day Ketogenic Cleanse*, Emmerich offers readers a day-by-day guide to what they should eat and when they should eat it. Foods include Snickerdoodle Waffles, Breakfast Chili, Bacon and Eggs Ramen, Chocolate Pudding, Chicken Neapolitan, Asian Pulled Pork Lettuce Cups, Spicy Grilled Shrimp, Bacon and Mushroom Burgers, Ethiopian Stew, Reuben Meatballs, Greek Avgolemono, Tom Ka Gai Chicken, Chicken Tinga

Wings,Lemon Pepper Wings, and Hot and Sour Soup with Pork Meatballs.

Discussion Questions

"Get Ready to Enter a New World"

Tip: Begin with questions dealing with broader issues to ensure ample time for quality discussions. Read through all discussion questions before engaging.

~~~

question 1

The food someone eats often tells a lot about a
person. What do you think your "typical" diet says
about you?

~~~

~~~

question 2

Maria Emmerich includes recipes in *The 30 Day Ketogenic Cleanse*. Why do you think she has chosen to do this?

~~~

~~~

question 3

In *The 30 Day Ketogenic Cleanse*, Maria Emmerich gives readers a meal plan they can follow for the keto cleanse. Why do you think she has included this food guide?

~~~

question 4

The title of this book is *The 30 Day Ketogenic Cleanse*.. What does Emmerich mean by a ketogenic cleanse?

~~~

question 5

The 30 Day Ketogenic Cleanse is a guide to the ketogenic diet. What originally drew you into this book and made you want to read it?

~~~

~~~

question 6

The 30 Day Ketogenic Cleanse is aimed at readers who want to try or retry the ketogenic diet. How well did this book live up to your expectations?

~~~

~~~

question 7

The ketogenic diet is the topic of *The 30 Day Ketogenic Cleanse*. Did you try the ketogenic diet after reading this book? Why or why not? What were your results?

~~~

~~~

question 8

There are thousands of diet books in the world. What makes *The 30 Day Ketogenic Cleanse* unique and stand out from the rest?

~~~

~~~

question 9

Maria Emmerich makes numerous health and diet claims in *The 30 Day Ketogenic Cleanse*. How believable was this information in your opinion?

~~~

~ ~ ~

question 10

In the ketogenic diet, there are foods that should be consumed and foods that should not be consumed, according to Maria Emmerich. What are your thoughts on these foods that should or should not be consumed?

~ ~ ~

question 11

The ketogenic diet is a diet that is high in fat and low in carbohydrates. What are your overall thoughts on this diet after learning more about it?

question 12

The 30 Day Ketogenic Cleanse explains a diet that is high fat and low carb. How does this diet differ from your current diet?

~~~

~~~

question 13

Maria Emmerich believes that the ketogenic diet will work for everyone. How true do you think this statement is?

~~~

question 14

The 30 Day Ketogenic Cleanse discusses many benefits of following this diet. What would be the greatest benefit of this diet to you?

~ ~ ~

question 15

The 30 Day Ketogenic Cleanse claims to reset a person's metabolism and heal their body from poor eating habits. How possible to you think this is?

~~~

~~~

question 16

Several readers have stated that the recipes in *The 30 Day Ketogenic Cleanse* are complicated. What are your thoughts on the recipes in this book?

~~~

~ ~ ~

question 17

One reader felt as though the information in *The 30 Day Ketogenic Cleanse* was written clearly and easy to understand, while another reader wanted more in depth explanations. How did you feel about the information presented in the book?

~ ~ ~

question 18

In the opinion of a reader of *The 30 Day Ketogenic Cleanse,* Emmerich included too much mindfulness, and it made it seem as though this was essential to having success with the ketogenic diet. What were your thoughts, overall, on how the book was written?

~ ~ ~

question 19

One reader pointed out that Emmerich talks about fasting for most days of the week in *The 30 Day Ketogenic Cleanse.* This reader felt as though the book is more of an anti-eating book than a book on how to eat healthily.

~~~

~~~

question 20

After reading *The 30 Day Ketogenic Cleanse*, several readers felt as though the ketogenic diet was not right for them. How did you feel about the ketogenic diet after reading?

~~~

Introducing the Author

Maria Emmerich is best known for her work as a researcher, author, and creator of recipes. Emmerich studied exercise science and nutrition for her college degree. However, she says most of her education was based on the food pyramid. Emmerich says she spent her childhood eating mainly whole grains, which were presented to her as healthy food options. Along with eating whole grains, Emmerich also ate foods that were low in fat. During this time, she was also overweight, and something inside of her told her that the way she was eating was incorrect. She knew that there must be a different, better way to eat that could help her be more healthy and lose weight. For about a decade, Emmerich devoted her life to researching health and food and writing books on these topics.

After researching scientific studies about food and health for many years, Emmerich found the ketogenic diet. Emmerich explains that the ketogenic diet is the closest diet to what the early ancestors of humans would eat. Further, Emmerich says the ketogenic diet is about eating the right ratio of carbs, fats, and proteins. According to Emmerich's research, this creates an environment in the human body that lowers inflammations. This helps people lose weight and helps the body recover from years of improper eating. In addition,

Emmerich's research has shown that eating in this way can help many different health issues. Some of these issues include Colitis, Crohn's Disease, other gastrointestinal issues, metabolic syndrome, auto immune diseases, alopecia, eczema, and acne. It is the belief of Emmerich that many conditions that seem impossible, or near impossible, to cure can be healed if people receive the right nutrients and supplements in their diets.

Maria Emmerich has written many cookbooks that help people eat nutrient-rich meals, while staying away from foods that are harming their health. In addition to her cookbooks, Emmerich has also written books that discuss health and nutrition. One of these books is *Keto-Adapted*. In this book,

Emmerich helps people who are interested in following a ketogenic diet make the lifestyle change. She provides readers with all of the tools that they need in order to transition to a ketogenic lifestyle. In the book, she also includes all of the data she has amassed over the years to show readers how eating a ketogenic diet is healthy for healing current health issues and how it can reduce the risk of serious health issues later in life.

In addition to her health books for adults, she has also written a book aimed at helping children eat healthier. This book is called *The Art of Healthy Eating: Kids*. Emmerich was inspired to write this book because she is aware that children are given so many unhealthy food options at school, and often these food choices are processed. Because of this, Emmerich has made the decision to home school her children. This way she can keep them on a ketogenic diet. She is also able to give them a better education about food choices and how they affect the human body later in life.

Health and nutrition are one of the biggest passions for Maria Emmerich. She often gets emails from people who are following her and listening to her health advice. These people are seeing major turnarounds in their health. They are loosing hundreds of pounds, reversing diabetes, gastrointestinal issues, autoimmune diseases, and skin issues. This drives her and makes her want to help more people. She says it is gratifying for her that she has been able to help people become healthier and get off of their medications simply by eating a proper diet.

Bonus Downloads
*Get Free Books with **Any Purchase** of* Conversation Starters!

Every purchase comes with a FREE download!

Add spice to any conversation
Never run out of things to say
Spend time with those you love

Get it Now

or Click Here.

Scan Your Phone

Fireside Questions

"What would you do?"

Tip: These questions can be a fun exercise as it spurs creativity among the readers by allowing alternate scene endings and "if this was you" questions.

question 21

Maria Emmerich has decided to keep her children at home so that they can follow a ketogenic diet. What are your thoughts on this decision?

~ ~ ~

question 22

In the opinion of Maria Emmerich, people can heal the effects of many illnesses by following a ketogenic diet. What do you think of these claims?

~ ~ ~

question 23

Maria Emmerich says it is gratifying for her to know that people are becoming healthier because of her work. Why do you think this is so important to her?

~~~

~~~

question 24

As a child, Maria Emmerich was bullied for her weight. How do you think this experience shaped her future?

~~~

~~~

question 25

Maria Emmerich made the decision to change her diet after college. Why do you think she made this decision?

~~~

~~~

question 26

The 30 Day Ketogenic Cleanse offers diet advice to readers. What diet advice would you give to people?

~~~

question 27

Maria Emmerich has done extensive research on diets and how they relate to health. What area of health would you like to research?

~ ~ ~

question 28

In order to keep her children on a healthy diet, Maria Emmerich has chosen to homeschool her children. Would you have done the same?

~~~

question 29

In addition to writing health books, Maria Emmerich also writes cookbooks. What recipes would you put in a cookbook?

~ ~ ~

~~~

question 30

The 30 Day Ketogenic Cleanse is a book designed to help people start the ketogenic diet. What would you add or take out of this book to improve it?

~~~

Quiz Questions

"Ready to Announce the Winners?"

Tip: Create a leaderboard and track scores to see who gets the most correct answers. Winners required. Prizes optional.

~~~

quiz question 1

The 30 Day Ketogenic Cleanse is the newest book by Maria Emmerich. It is designed to help people through the first 30 days of the ketogenic diet, which are often the most _____.

~~~

quiz question 2

The ketogenic diet is built upon the idea that the body will burn fat, which are also called _____, when the person is eating proper foods. In addition, the energy should come from protein and fats rather than carbohydrates.

quiz question 3

In the first 30 days, the body can have a difficult time adapting to the new way of eating. This often leads to _____ and people generally feeling unwell.

~ ~ ~

quiz question 4

In addition to providing information about the ketogenic diet, there is also a meal plan along with _____. They are designed to be satisfying to help the reader with cravings while they are adapting to the lifestyle change.

~ ~ ~

quiz question 5

True or False: Maria Emmerich was inspired to write this book because of her experiences in childhood. Emmerich was overweight as a child and bullied because of this.

quiz question 6

True or False: Before starting the ketogenic diet, Maria Emmerich thought that eating fats was unhealthy. Now, she knows that fats are healthy and carbohydrates should be limited.

quiz question 7

True or False: Maria Emmerich does not have any scientific evidence to back up why the ketogenic diet works. She only knows from her own experiences.

~~~

quiz question 8

Maria Emmerich studied exercise science and
_____ for her college degree.
However, she says most of this education was
based around the food pyramid, which she no
longer believes is an accurate model for nutrition.

quiz question 9

During her youth, Emmerich struggled with her weight. She had a feeling that the way she was eating was incorrect, and devoted a decade into _____ health and food.

quiz question 10

According to Emmerich's research, the ketogenic diet can help the human body lower _____. In turn, this can heal the body from a number of major illnesses.

~ ~ ~

quiz question 11

True or False: Maria Emmerich has also written books aimed at helping children eat healthy. Emmerich says that the options children have for food are often unhealthy and can lead to health problems later in life.

quiz question 12

True or False: The biggest passions for Maria Emmerich are health and nutrition. She says it is gratifying for her when people have seen their health turn around because of her advice.

Quiz Answers

1. Difficult
2. Ketones
3. Cravings
4. Recipes
5. True
6. True
7. False
8. Nutrition
9. Researching
10. Inflammation
11. True
12. True

Ways to Continue Your Reading

E VERY month, our team runs through a wide selection of books to pick the best titles for readers and reading groups, and promotes these titles to our thousands of readers – sometimes with free downloads, sale dates, and additional brochures.

Click here to sign up for these benefits.

If you have not yet read the original work or would like to read it again, you can purchase the original book here.

Bonus Downloads
*Get Free Books with **Any Purchase** of Conversation Starters!*

Every purchase comes with a FREE download!

Add spice to any conversation
Never run out of things to say
Spend time with those you love

Get it Now

or Click Here.

Scan Your Phone

On the Next Page...

If you found this book helpful to your discussions and rate it a 4 or 5, please write us a review on the next page.

Any length would be fine but we'd appreciate hearing you more! We'd be very encouraged.

Till next time,

BookHabits

"Loving Books is Actually a Habit"